And Beyond

Rae Gunn

BookLeaf
Publishing

India | USA | UK

Presentation by *BookLeaf Publishing*

Web: www.bookleafpub.com

E-mail: info@bookleafpub.com

ISBN: 9789357443326

First edition 2022

DEDICATION

To my husband, Chad, for being such a driving force in my life. I love you. Forever and Always.

To my children, Cielle and Clark, you are my heaven and earth. My greatest accomplishments, and the only art I completed in creating prior to this book.

PREFACE

I wrote these poems in times when I felt like an outsider. Whether it be from my disabilities or from my identity as a nonbinary, asexual, polyamorous, parent and spouse. I've been through traumas and heartaches that have shaped my views of the universe around me. My hope is that some of these resonate with you, Dear Reader, even if our paths are not similar.

And Beyond

It's not just in the way you look at me,
It's the way you look past all the terrible things I
see in myself.
And it's not just how you hold my hand,
But how you hold me together when I'm falling
apart.
It's not just the way your smile lights the room,
But how you never leave me alone in the dark.
Your lips may kiss deep,
But how you inspire me goes deeper.

And When the stars burn out
When our planet grows cold
When the weight of the universe collapses itself,
My love for you will remain.

The Usual Bedtime Routine

Sometimes I find my mind drifting
It always starts slowly
A past event, a distant memory.

The sounds become louder,
The lights become brighter,
Every touch becomes treachery.

Inhale. Exhale. Inhale. Inhale.
No order to my breathing,
Heartbeat pounding like drums.

Ever increasing in speed.
My body clammy and shaking.
The high pitched overwhelming hums.

Generalized anxiety
Existential dread.

Two Metres Away

I keep, scrolling and scrolling
Trying to keep the connections going
Except I'm not really knowing
When to stop

We've all been 2 meters apart
Missing out on ends and starts
Feeling heavy in our hearts
For too long

We kept thinking it'd be gone
Now it's delta and omicron
And more rules are redrawn
To get ahead

I'm hoping one day soon
When we gather off Zoom
And our faces are free from the masks
That we'll finally see
The end of covid-19
And the new normal we made can last

I Wish I Had An Umbrella

Mercury might be in retrograde
My serotonin is man-made
I've got executive dysfunction
So much fear and compunction
I'm your average Millennial
Feeling extraterrestrial
Hearing Boomers chastise us
Laughs in housing crisis
Over educated and underpaid
Living with stagnant pay grades
Turning hobbies into hustles
Stop minimizing the struggles
Tired of the daily grind
Being forced into a hive mind
Survived "once in a lifetime"
More than enough times
We're perpetually "kids"
Because student debt still lives
But we're reaching middle age
THIS IS NOT JUST A PHASE

Tiny Humans

To my first born child,
You are stronger than you know
I thank you for your patience
As our family has grown

I know some days you're jealous
Or feeling a bit left out
While we rock your sibling
You sit and pout

But you're bigger and older
And wise beyond years
Bringing soothers and diapers
Shushing away baby's tears

And once they're asleep
We can snuggle and play
I love you, my first baby
Forever and a day

Spiralling

There are days when I'm utterly exhausted.
When it feels like an insurmountable task just to
shower.

When the light from my window signals
morning,
But I still haven't managed to fall asleep.

Endless loops of chores and responsibilities,
And I can't seem to find the willpower.

I'm too busy taking care of others,
That I didn't even remember to eat.

And just when I think I'm not enough,
That's when the village steps up

Tears Water Your Garden

The blood of your enemies
Is great for growing flowers
So bloom where you're planted
And show them your powers
Sprout tall and wild
Let no one cut you back
Don't worry your worth
Your petals don't lack

Participation Awards

I would love to be the runner-up.
Because from my spot; it's an impossible wish.
First place gets the fame, the glory, their name in
lights.
Second place gets the recognition, the grace of
mistakes.
Runner-ups get the support, and that's what
matters most.
The "you can do it!l And "we'll get 'em next
time."
The chants and cheers from the crowd are
loudest for those at the back of the race.
"Keep going, don't give up!"
"You did your best, we love you!"

Being runner-up isn't the worst.
The worst is when you're forgotten all together.

Watchtower Of The East

The wind is a beautiful power
Strong enough to tear down houses
As if they were simply cardboard
Yet gentle enough to carry
The seeds of rebirth
Howling like a grieving widow
Or whispers like a sneaky child
Sharp like wild teeth
Or soft as a baby's breath
It can bring relief
From unforgiving heat
Or it can be the devastation
That brings a town to its knees
It's a wonder and a fright
To listen on a stormy night

My Friend The Dark

There is comfort in the dark
When you listen to your heart
And find that inner spark
Know you play a greater part

There is peace in the shadows
When things fall like dominoes
And you're left with what you chose
Make sure your light shows

There is hope in the abyss
When you grieving those you miss
And you sit and reminisce
Give those memories a kiss

There is grace in the void
When everything seems destroyed
And you barely feel humanoid
Let your heart be overjoyed

Because there is comfort in the dark.

Personal Growth

Who you once were is important
It was a stepping stone to who you are now
Did you make mistakes?
Were you always kind and fair?
Those moments helped you grow
Let you find a better self
And years from now
When you're old and gray
You'll be different than you are today

It Gets Better

Home isn't always the safe space we need
Sometimes it's neglectful and cold
Or hostile and mean
But I promise it gets better if you hold on
Pick your family
And surround yourself with support
Find your place in the world
And get a running start
Blood means nothing
If it doesn't fill your heart

Nights Like These

Your breath smells of whiskey and lime
Your head between your pillow and mine
Eyes closed tightly, dreaming
Light snores, deep breathing
These moments are fleeting
Listening to your heart beating
Strong hands, gentle touch
I love you so much.

A Flower Amongst The Weeds

A rose didn't ask to grow thorns
They evolved out of necessity
To protect the delicate petals
And defend the beauty they hold
You didn't ask for your thorns either
You adapted to your situation
Protected yourself from harm
You guarded your petals
From unwanted attention
And your softness comes with a sting
But some day you'll find someone
Who can prune you without pain
And aid you to flourish and grow
To keep your roots deep
And your colours to glow
A gardener to call your own

She Tried

She hides all the clouds
And she steals all the stars
Because nothing should be beautiful
When her heart is full of scars

The pain in her soul
Runs deep and cold
When the world turns away
And words burn too bold

Like a sunflower turns
To the light of the sun
She looked for brightness
But always found none

She took her life before she knew
If things would change tomorrow
And now she sleeps forever
In the Garden of Sorrow

RIP R.J.

Spectrum

Those two little eyes look up at me.
They see no flaws, no mediocrity.
Only safety, grace, and love.
A chest of comfort to dream of.
I may be divergent of the norm,
But they only know my warmth.
My lumps and edges aren't too much,
When all they need is my touch.
What does it mean to be queer?
That 5 letter word I endear.
My body doesn't define my role,
Loving them is my only goal.

Finally

Finally.
Finally I am breaking out of this chrysalis.
No more am I a blob of my former self.
I've grown my wings and can take to the sky.
Finally.

Finally I am strong enough to move mountains.
I can understand these changes.
Push myself to my boundaries and respect my
limitations.
Finally.

Finally has finally come.

To Infinity

Here's to the moments we hold on to.
The memories we replay.
The photos we always flip through.
And the laughter that we made.

Here's to the nights that never ended,
And the days that last forever.
We'd talk for hours and hours,
And take off to wherever.

Here's to the moments that took our breath away.
Or made us shed a tear.
Those points stay with us always.
As we journey through the years.

Here's to infinity.
You and I.

www.ingramcontent.com/pod-product-compliance
Lightning Source LLC
LaVergne TN
LVHW050300200726
843509LV00015B/3073